A Guide to the Art of Musical Performance

A Guide to the Art of Musical Performance

A Guide to the Art
of
Musical Performance

by

Kenneth P. Langer

A Guide to the Art of Musical Performance
by Kenneth P. Langer

Version 1.02
Expanded and Revised
published by
Brass Bell Books
www.brassbellbooks.com

ISBN: 978-1-329-90607-5

Produced in the United States of America
The author may be contacted at ken.langer@me.com

Introduction

This work began as a textbook for class entitled Performance Workshop which was required for all music majors in my program. Performance Workshop was designed to help students become better solo and ensemble musical performers (regardless of musical style) through dedicated practice and critiques of performances done before the class. Developing as a better musician requires developing, practicing, performing, and evaluating musical techniques and methods. This text provides suggestions for accomplishing these things.

Table of Contents

Table of Contents

A Guide to the Art of Musical Performance

Solo Practice Techniques

Reasons For Practicing

<u>The Purpose of Practice</u>

To develop technique

To learn music

To memorize music

To develop an interpretation

To prepare for a performance

To some, practicing music is viewed as a drudgery and a nuisance when compared to the joy of live performing. After all, people want to learn music so they can enjoy playing but performing on any instrument (in this book, the voice will be considered an instrument as well) requires hours of careful practice and evaluation in order for a musician to be skilled enough to perform well. On average, it takes at least ten years of consistent and dedicated practice to develop the skills needed to be an accomplished performing musician.

There are several reasons you should commit yourself to a consistent and productive practice routine. These reasons include: developing technique with your instrument, to learn new music, to memorize musical pieces, to develop an interpretation of a piece of music, and to prepare for a specific performance.

All musicians need to be proficient with their instrument. Every musical instrument has its own peculiar quirks and challenges, requiring the musician to develop techniques to overcome these challenges and make beautiful sounds. Developing as a musician is not that different from developing as an athlete. Take bike riding, for example. Most any person of standard physical structure can ride a bike up and down the street but it takes special skill, knowledge, and technique to learn to race a bike in a competition. The rider must intimately know the idiosyncrasies of the bike and how to ride it in order to gain optimum performance. Doing this requires hours of practice in different environments. The best riders make racing bikes look easy and beautiful but such grace is only possible after years of careful training. The same is true of developing musical skill. The musician must know the instrument and how to produce the best sounds with ease and clarity. He or she must be able to successfully take on any musical challenge and make the results sound beautiful and clear.

One of those challenges is learning to be able to sight read music quickly and efficiently so that the time needed to learn new pieces is reduced to a bare minimum. Professional musicians are hired on their ability to make beautiful music but also on their ability to quickly pass the learning stage of any piece of music. They need to be able to effectively and quickly sight read to be hired. Learning to sight read will also make your practice sessions more efficient. If you can quickly get past the stage of learning a new piece of music, then you will have more time to actually shape and refine its performance.

Sometimes music needs to be memorized for performances. This is especially true for vocal performers and pianists. Practice time can be used to learn and memorize music. Some people try to memorize music by constantly repeating the whole piece over and over again. This is usually an ineffective way to memorize anything. Research has shown that we tend to memorize in small chunks. Musical phrases are often the perfect length for memorization, so the first step in memorizing a piece of music is to determine the structure of the piece by observing its phrases. Phrases are like musical sentences or individual ideas in any kind of music. If you can memorize one phrase at a time and then link those phrases together, you will memorize in a quick and efficient fashion.

Interpretation is when a musician adds his or her own personal flair or style to a piece of music. No one wants to go to a performance to hear someone play someone else's music played the same way every time. Each performer can add a fresh perspective or individual style to any piece of music by developing a personal interpretation of that piece. Practice time is needed to experiment with style and to find a performance of that piece that is both unique and interesting while still true to the concepts originally intended in the music.

Probably the most important purpose of developing a regular and effective practice routine is to prepare for a performance. The performance of music can be the moment when you shine or it can be a nerve-racking and frightening experience. Practicing a piece of music helps to insure that you perform it at a high degree of quality and aesthetic effectiveness. You should strive to practice a performance piece to the point that you feel highly confident about the performance. In effect, you should work to "over-practice" the music so that you will be prepared for any mishap or panic that may set in.

Preparation For Practicing

Practice Preparation

Establish a regular routine

Prepare your space and yourself to practice

Set clear goals

Work toward those goals

An effective practice session needs to be carefully prepared, planned, and executed so that it can be as efficient as possible. Just playing through all the music over and over again from start to finish is not an effective use of your time and talent.

To prepare yourself for a well designed practice session you should: establish a regular practice place and time, eliminate all disturbances from your practice area, relax yourself physically and mentally, set out some clear goals for your practice session, and plan out your practice so that your goals are met in determined time frames.

One of the most important ways to develop good practice habits is to develop a consistent routine for practice. You should develop a schedule that allows you to practice for at least an hour, and for at least three days a week. It is best to repeat that same weekly schedule as often as possible so that the schedule becomes a habit for you. The place and time in which you practice should be free of all distractions. Turn off all unnecessary devices and set aside the practice time for yourself and your music.

Before beginning any music routines, try to get as relaxed as possible. Just like an athlete needs to relax and warm up before adding any strain to their muscles, so the musician needs to do the same. Playing any instrument or singing involves applying a heavy strain to a number of small muscles. If those muscles are not relaxed and stretched beforehand, the additional strain could cause temporary or permanent damage. Find some exercises you can do to relax and stretch those muscles before playing. It is also important to relax mentally before beginning any practice session. Block out all the stress and strain brought on by the day and prepare yourself to focus only on making music.

It is important that all practice sessions be more than just playing through pieces of music. Getting better as a musician requires many years of not just practice but of effective practice that allows you to build on learned techniques and skills in an efficient manner. An effective rehearsal requires planning and execution. You should set out one to three clear goals for your practice session. These should be based on long term musical goals that you have established for yourself. Each practice session gives you a chance to focus on a small part of your long term goals. A short term goal devised for each practice session makes it possible to reach the long term goals. Plan out your practice to determine what specifically you wish to accomplish and create detailed objectives that can be met in that rehearsal. Decide how much time you want to devote to each objective and plan accordingly.

<u>An example of a long term goal</u>

Goal: To increase my upper range of playing or singing

An example of a short term goal that can be used in a practice session to meet the long term goal:

Goal: To increase my comfortable upper range by one additional note by working up to it slowly.

Five Parts of an Effective Practice Session

The Practice Session

Warm-up

Read new music

Work on exercises

Work on prepared music

Warm-down

An effective practice includes more than just playing music. It needs to include things that will help you develop as a musician and prepare you to meet any musical challenge you may face in the future. There are five things that every practice session should include to help you reach these larger goals. Those five things are: warm-ups, sight reading exercises, musical exercises, musical work, and warm-downs.

The first part of every practice session should be the warm-up. This is the part of the practice where you should concentrate on relaxing and preparing your muscles and your mind so that you will be ready to play music without physical and mental distractions. Relax and stretch before playing. Then start playing some very easy exercises such as scales and long notes to help prepare the specific muscles involved in playing. The warm-up time is not a chance to develop technique or improve your playing ability. The focus on the warm-up should be on centering in on the practice session and playing with a good, clear, and strong tone with a minimum of effort.

Playing or singing long tones are an excellent way to warm up.

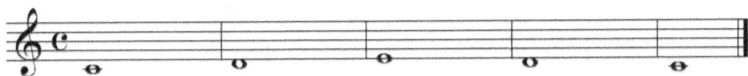

After playing long tones, some faster playing can be done to further warm-up. Playing or singing scales is a good way to accomplish this goal.

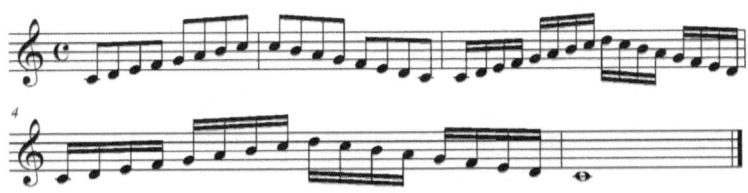

All practice sessions should also include sight reading exercises. Unfortunately for many developing musicians, sight reading is often neglected. Sight reading, however, is one of a professional musician's most important skills. Being able to read new music quickly and efficiently reduces the need for extensive time dedicated to learning the music and allows for more time to be spent on shaping and perfecting the music instead. Every practice session should include time for taking a piece of music never seen before and reading through it to develop better reading abilities. There are many other sources such as books and online materials that can be found to provide sight reading practice.

Next, an effective practice session should include specific musical exercises that are designed to challenge your ability and develop your technique. Just like someone training to lift weights or do gymnastics would start with small challenges and then increase the difficulty of those challenges, so the musician must do the same. There are many books and other sources that have exercises designed to develop specific skills. These may be called exercises or etudes but the concept is the same. To use these exercises, you should determine what specific ability you wish to develop, then find exercises to help with the development and improvement of that skill. You should know the exact goal for each exercise you play. Then, determine how that exercise is trying to get you to improve that skill. When practicing the exercise, do not simply play straight through it hoping for a different result each time. Work to make progress on specific parts of the exercise and then play it through all the way. You need to demand the best from yourself in order to get the best. Sometimes it can be helpful to actually design your own musical exercises based on other exercises or on parts of a piece of music you know needs work.

<u>Steps for Preparing Music</u>

Look through the whole piece or potential problems

Play through the whole piece once or twice

Practice the problem areas in isolation

Put the piece together

Most people include in their practice sessions some music that they know they need to work on for an upcoming performance. The problem is that many musicians simply play through the music from top to bottom without actually trying to make a detailed effort to play it any better. Here are some steps to help make practicing music more efficient: look over the whole piece first before playing it to determine its overall structure, play through the whole piece once or twice, find and practice problem areas, then put the piece together and play the whole thing again.

First, look through the entire piece of music to try and get an idea of what it is all about and where it is going. Here is where knowledge of music theory can be helpful in analyzing what is happening in the music. You will want to pay special attention to those places that have repeated material. It is a waste of time to play repeated sections over and over again. Instead, once you have mastered a particular section, skip ahead to new material in the music. When you have finished looking over the whole piece, then play through the whole thing but only once or twice. Take note in the music or in your head where you had specific problems. Practice just those problem areas until you have mastered them before repeating the whole piece or even a whole section again. Sometimes it is helpful to create your own musical exercises based on the musical challenges you encountered during practice so that the next time you run into a similar challenge you can easily overcome it. When you have mastered all the difficult sections, put it all together and play through the whole piece so that you can establish a complete flow of motion from the beginning to the end.

The last part of a successful rehearsal should include time for warm-downs. Many musicians have heard the term warm-ups but less have heard the term warm-downs. These are things you do at the end of the rehearsal to help you relax after a tough session and to help you feel good about what you have done. Warm-downs are the opposite of warm-ups. When you have finished playing a lot of music you will probably feel tired and tense. You should take some time to try and relax and stretch your muscles out once again. Loosen yourself up physically and mentally as well. This is the time to play something you know well and enjoy so that your rehearsal ends on a positive note. Also, take some time to evaluate your practice. Take note of things you need to improve upon but also take note of the things you did well. At the end of your practice you should feel relaxed, refreshed, and know that you have done some good work.

Ensemble Practice Techniques

Many of the same techniques that can be applied to developing a successful practice routine for a single musician can also be applied to a musical ensemble with some additional considerations. In general, some groups like orchestras, choirs, or large bands, will be led by a single individual. That person is in charge of directing rehearsals and performances for the entire ensemble. Some groups, however, like small jazz ensembles and contemporary rock bands do not have a single assigned leader. Rather, direction is spread out among the members. This can be difficult, however, for the entire group to find a single course of action for rehearsing and practicing. In such cases, either a single leader needs to be identified or a method of fairly distributing responsibility among the members of the group needs to be determined. This process must take place with the agreement of all the members at the beginning of any series of rehearsals. Having such an agreement in place will avoid many possible arguments and disagreements (hopefully!).

If the group is led by a single leader, that person can provide a focus for the rest of the group. That person's vision of how the music will be performed should be clearly outlined to the group and the leader should strive to make that vision a reality. That vision will be the director's own interpretation of how the music should be done to make the performance unique and interesting.

Leaders can plan and direct rehearsals making sure that they stay on track and follow a plan to work toward the performance goal.

Sometimes having a single director can be useful and productive since it can cut down on the number of disagreements on style and interpretation. Some groups, however, desire to work on a more egalitarian level. This allows for the input of all the members but, in the end, the group has to come to a decision on a single vision–whether it be of one person or from a collaboration. A single vision is the only way that a group can attempt to work together.

The Rehearsal Schedule

When a director is in charge of setting a rehearsal schedule for a group, there are several factors that need to be considered. First, the director must know when there will be a performance and what musical pieces will be performed on that date. At that point the director should determine how many rehearsals there will be until the performance. Next, the director should estimate how much time will be needed to practice and polish each of the pieces. The music should be prioritized in terms of its difficulty with the work of the greatest difficulty on top. Rehearsal should then be planned with approximate timings showing how much time will be spent on each piece of music.

The Successful Rehearsal

Group Rehearsal
Group discussion
Tune together
Warm-ups
Rehearse
Warm-downs

A successful rehearsal should begin with a brief group discussion in which the goals and expectations for that rehearsal should be clearly explained. It is important for each member of the ensemble to know what it is they hope to accomplish and what they will be doing during the rehearsal. Once the goals have been set, the group should be tuned together. Each member of the ensemble should already have warmed up and tuned their own instrument before beginning the rehearsal but the whole group also needs to tune together.

Most orchestras and classical music groups tune to a standard pitch of "A" at 440 beats per second (A=440). Once the group is tuned, the director should lead them in some simple warm-ups. Although individual members may have warmed up before the rehearsal, group warm-ups help to get the ensemble to play together and in sync. The group should then begin rehearsing the music according to the goals and schedule set out by the director, or the group as a whole. Just before practice ends, the group should then play some simple and fun music together to warm-down and end the rehearsal on a positive note. After all, the group is not only there to work, they want to enjoy their music-making as well.

Solo and Ensemble Performance Techniques

Solo Performance Techniques

What makes for a good performance? Certainly it is about "getting it right" but just playing the music correctly is not enough to make a truly good performance. Playing the music correctly is only the beginning of developing a great musical performance. Somehow, a performer must go deeper than that. In fact, a performer must go two levels deeper.

There are three levels of musical performance: accuracy, musicality, and passion.

Three Levels of Musical Performance
Accuracy
Musicality
Passion

Accuracy

At the level of accuracy, the first level of performance, the performer learns to play all the notes and rhythms correctly in the context of the style of the music being performed. The performer also learns to play those notes with a beautiful tone and with pitches that are in tune. A classical musician learns to play the notes and rhythms written out on a score while a contemporary or folk musician learns to play notes and rhythms according to a tradition. Accuracy is the first level because nothing else can be added to the performance until the notes and rhythms are learned but they must be more than just learned, they must be set deep into the psyche and the muscle memory of the performer so that he or she can take the music to the next level.

Musicality

The second level of performance is called musicality or shaping. It is how the actual notes and rhythms are played. A technical performance is one in which everything is played correctly but a technical performance is not necessarily one that people enjoy hearing. There is a subtlety that needs to be added to those notes and rhythms to make them interesting. This shaping can be done through several methods including dynamics, articulations, tempo changes, and phrasing. Other methods include a change of timbre (instrumentation) and changes in tone color such as through the use of vibrato and tone quality.

Dynamics are levels of volume in music. There are both macro-dynamics and micro-dynamics. Macro-dynamics are large scale changes in volume such as when a phrase begins softly but then increases in volume or vice versa. Large scale dynamics can cover an entire piece, individual phrases, or small sections of the music. Micro-dynamics are changes in volume at the level of the individual note. Single notes or small groups of notes can have dynamic changes that make their performance more interesting.

Examples of dynamics

piano - soft volume

forte - loud voume

crescendo - get gradually louder

decrescendo - get gradually softer

Individual notes can also be played in different ways. These are called articulations (micro-dynamics) and can include things like attacks, lengthening of the note (legato), shortening of the note (staccato), and other subtle changes in volume. Each of these add movement and interest and can make the performance seem more alive.

Examples of microdynamics

accent - a strong attack on a note

marcato - to give a full sound to a note

sforzando - a strong attack with a long decay

fortepiano - to play a note first at a forte volume

then change to a piano volume.

Examples of other types of articulations

staccato - play the note short

legato - play the note long

Tempo, or the speed of the music, can also add shape and interest. Large sections or even phrases can be made to speed up or slow down to make the music have more movement to it. Changes in tempo can be over long or short periods of time and sudden changes in tempo such as through rhythmic stops can add to the shaping of the music.

Phrasing is learning to play the music as an expression of ideas rather than as just a collection of notes. A phrase is the musical equivalent of a sentence. As you read these notes you see that there are words but they are grouped into sentences. The sentence is the idea created through the words. A phrase in music is a collection of notes put together to create a musical idea. Punctuation is used to set sentences apart. In music, punctuation is created by using rests, endings, cadences (specific chord patterns), long notes, and phrase markings (a long curved line set above the music). Learning to express these musical sentences is what makes interesting to hear.

Consider the following haiku

Tedious hillside.

A little feathered wren chirps,

Betrayed by the cow.

It is three lines long. Each line is a separate idea set apart by space and punctuation. Try reading the poem aloud as if it were one long sentence. Then, read it aloud as three separate ideas with some separation between each one. Your second reading should seem more effective and interesting. The same is true for music. Learn to identify phrases and other musical ideas so that you can express them effectively.

Passion

The third level of musical performance is called passion or energy. Unfortunately, many young performers never reach this stage and, instead, get stuck on accuracy and shaping but passion and energy are the very things that the audience craves most from a performance. A successful performance is one that moves the listeners emotionally. Adding energy to a performance is a purely personal contribution to the music. There are no notes in the score or instructions from the writer or composer on how exactly to feel the music. That has to come from the heart and has to be displayed fully and honestly to the audience. If energy is applied to an original work of music, it is called expressing the music. If the music is your own, you are free to express it however you like. If the music is originally by someone else, then adding interest and energy to the performance is called an interpretation. Interpretation has to be done by considering the original composer's or writer's intentions and then adding your own energy to the work as well. If the audience has heard your song or music before, they will be interested in how you personally approach the work and how you will bring your own energy, style, and musical experience to the performance.

Passion is applied to a performance by first making a personal connection to the music itself and the meaning and experience it was meant to convey. This is where a careful analysis of the music comes into play. (Yes, there is a purpose to music theory!) The more intimately a performer knows the work to be performed, the more a personal sense of style and finesse can be added to the performance. Professional actors often spend months or years getting to understand the character they are going to portray and they spend many hours reading and understanding the script and its many overt and subtle messages. The same must be true for a musical performance. A performer must know the music well enough to be able to perform it with energy. Once the performer knows the music and understands its musical and emotional goals, energy can be applied through the use of something called musical motion.

Musical Motion

Three Parts of Musical Motion
Stasis
Intensity
Resolution

Musical motion is created through three functions: stasis, intensity, and resolution. The first part in creating musical motion is to create stasis or a place of familiarity. Without a "home" base there will be nothing from which to diverge. You can compare musical motion to the motion of runners on a baseball diamond. They must always start on home plate. As they move around the bases to score a run they go further and further away from home plate until they reach second plate (intensity). On the way to third plate the runner starts to head back towards home and must reach home plate in order to score the run (resolution).

Stasis

Stasis is created by establishing familiarity and unity. It is the central pitch and harmony of the piece as well as familiar musical ideas that may be introduced. The beginning of most pieces of music is designed to create this sense of stasis. Central musical ideas are presented and often repeated so that the listener becomes familiar and comfortable with them. In a typical song, for example, the section called the chorus helps to create stasis. The chorus is the part of a song that is repeated throughout with the same music and the same words. This repetition helps to define the music and offers comfort through familiarity.

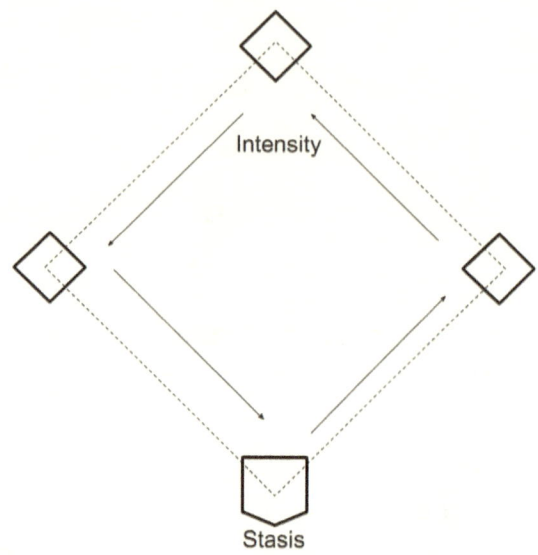

The same idea is true if you plan to go on vacation. When it is time to go you will leave the familiarity of your home and head to someplace different. When you arrive you may explore new places and try new things but, eventually, you will want to return back to your home where everything is familiar. In all forms of art, the artist must first create that sense of a place of familiarity and that is usually done early on in the presentation of the art form. In music it means presenting themes, motives, and other musical ideas through phrases that can be repeated so that they become known and familiar. Repetition is the key to stasis. What makes our home so familiar is that we have lived in it for many days and have seen, again and again, the same things. The same is true for art.

Repeating something–be it a melodic motive or theme, a harmonic sequence, a rhythmic pattern, or anything else–creates familiarity and develops a place for establishing home.

Intensity

A region of intensity is where the music builds toward more tension or moves away from the stasis usually created at the beginning. There are some specific ways that this tension can be created through music. Some of them are illustrated in the chart below. As intensity is increased, a push is often made to a climax or high point of the tension.

Creating Intensity		
pitches	*build toward*	non-tonic notes
low notes	*build toward*	high notes
long notes	*build toward*	short notes
consonant harmonies	*build toward*	dissonant harmonies
thin textures	*build toward*	thick textures
soft volumes	*build toward*	loud volumes

repetition	*build toward*	contrasting ideas
dark sounds	*build toward*	bright sounds
slow rhythms	*build toward*	fast rhythms

Here are some very simple musical examples of low intensity moving toward high intensity.

Applying Movement

Low moves to High

An ascending major scale with pitch intensity:

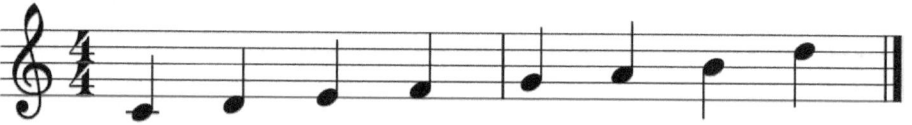

- The C major scale does not end on the tonic (C).

With rhythmic intensity:

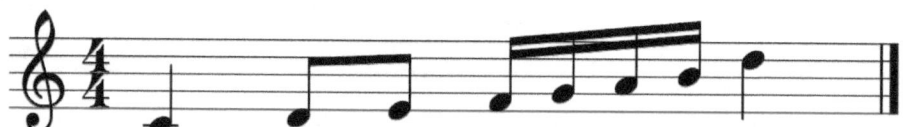

- The pitches move faster.

With dynamic intensity:

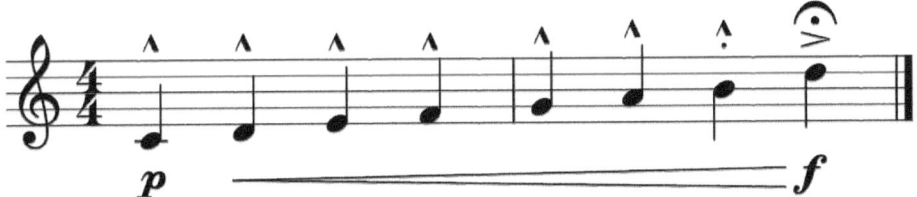

- The dynamic level changes from soft (p) to loud (f) with a crescendo.

- The articulations create even more movement.

With tempo intensity:

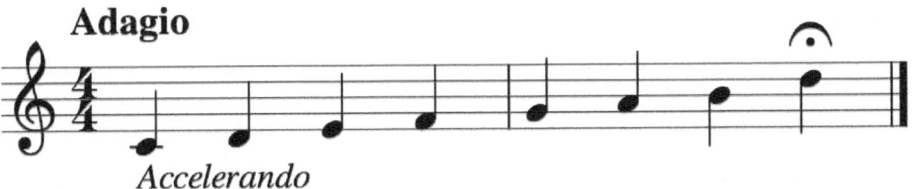

- The Adagio is a moderately slow tempo

- The accelerando means to get gradually faster.

- The fermata at the end also changes the tempo by elongating the final note's length.

Resolution

After stasis has been established and an intensity is built, there is usually a relaxing of tension through a short or long resolution phase. This motion is essentially in the opposite direction of intensity.

Creating Resolution		
pitches	*resolve toward*	tonic notes
high notes	*resolve toward*	low notes
short notes	*resolve toward*	long notes
dissonant harmonies	*resolve toward*	consonant harmonies
thick textures	*resolve toward*	thin textures
loud volumes	*resolve toward*	soft volumes
contrasting ideas	*resolve toward*	repetition
bright sounds	*resolve toward*	dark sounds
fast rhythms	*resolve toward*	slow rhythms

Here are some very simple musical examples of high intensity resolving towards low intensity.

Applying Movement

High moves to Low

A descending major scale with pitch resolution:

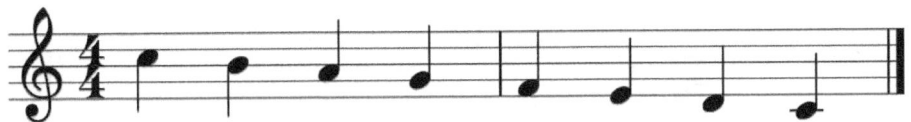

- The pitches of the C major scale resolve to tonic.

With rhythmic resolution:

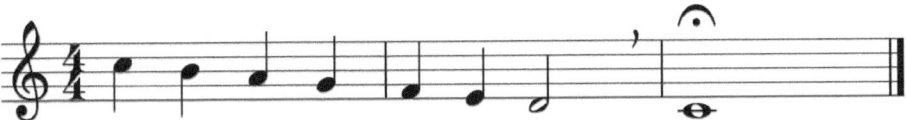

- The half note and the whole note slow down the rhythm.

- The breath mark in measure creates a pause.

With dynamic resolution:

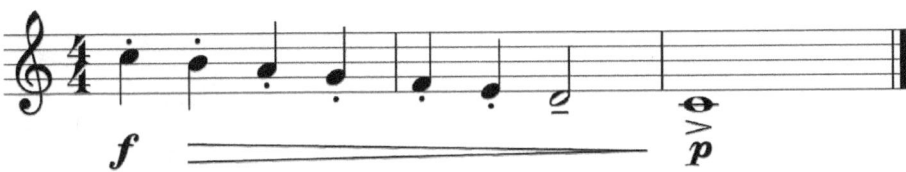

- The volume moves from loud (f) to soft (p) with a decrescendo.

- The articulations add more movement.

With tempo resolution:

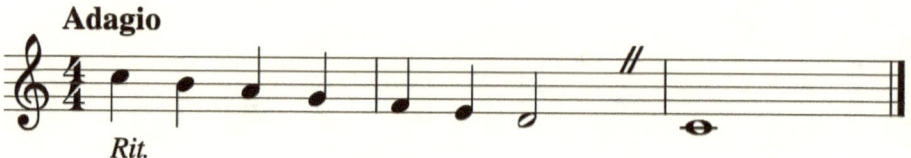

- Although the music starts moderately slow (Adagio) it is slowed even more with a ritard.

- The caesura in measure 2 creates a complete stop of the tempo.

Combining the Three (The Artistic Arch)

The movement of stasis, intensity, and resolution can be viewed in terms of a graph. High and Low points that move away from the static focus of the music create dramatic arches.

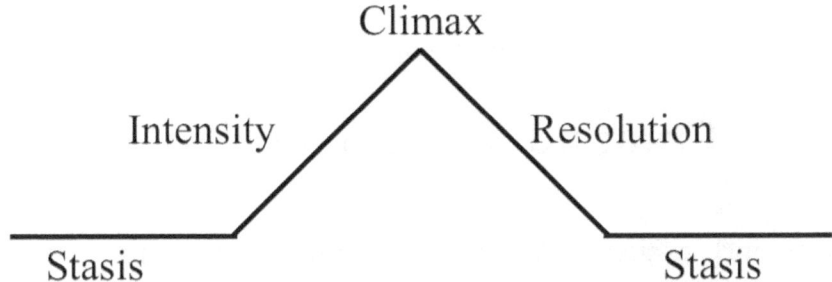

Sometimes, a piece of music will have multiple climactic points but, more often than not, one of those climactic points is meant to be greater than the others. The following illustration depicts several expansions, climactic points, and resolutions. The combination of these creates an overall arch of motion.

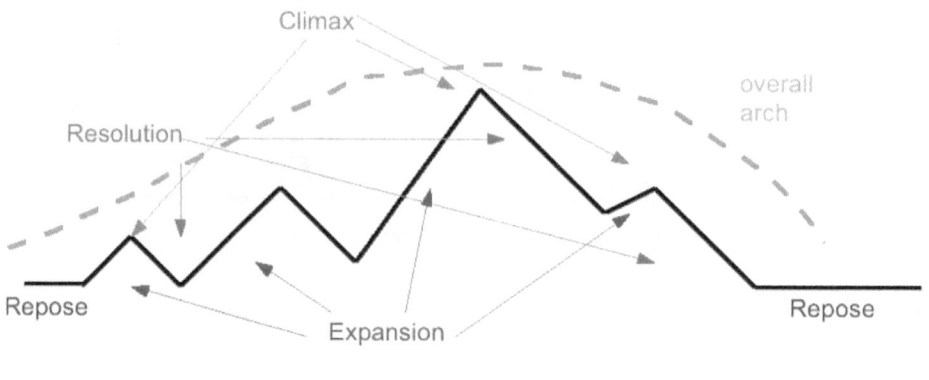

Illustration 7

Creating Musical Motion

Energy and excitement can be added to a performance by analyzing and then expressing the motion indicated or implied in the music itself. Determine how stasis is created. Look for the climactic points in the music and notice how they are approached and resolved. Practice the music so that these points and motions can all be brought out effectively to the audience.

Musical Expression

Another way to create interest in the performance is to connect the musical motion to different moods and emotional expressions. In the chart below, five examples of common human emotional moods are illustrated by using seven musical effects: tempo, dynamics, rhythm, articulation, timbre, vibrato, and rhythmic pauses.

	Tempo	Dynamics	Rhythm	Articulation	Timbre	Vibrato	Pauses
Happiness	fast, few changes	moderately loud	fast	marcato, variations	bright	small	few
Sadness	very slow, variations	soft	long notes, variations	legato	dark	slow	many
Anger	fast, few variations	loud	fast	staccato, heavy accents	bright, piercing	large	short
Tenderness	slow, few variations	moderately soft	long notes	legato, some accents	moderately soft	intense	slow

Fear	slow	very soft, much variation	long notes, much variation	staccato	bright	shallow	many

Using these examples you can explore how to use the second level of music performance–shaping–to help improve the third level of performance. The performer should experiment with these and other techniques to develop a highly expressive performance of a work of music. In effect, the musical performer is not much different from the actor who takes the stage and tries to convey a particular mood, theme, and emotional expression through words and actions.

Musical Interpretation

When you take music that has been composed by someone else but add your own particular ideas to its performance, that is called interpretation. There are a variety of ways of interpreting music including changing the shape of the music (dynamics, tempi, articulations, etc.) while another is to use musical elements of different styles.

Compare the following artists' renditions of the nursery song "Twinkle Twinkle Little Star." Each one provides a unique interpretation.

- Jewel (contemporary style)

- Frederika Stahl (folk style)

- Dead Space (electronic style)

- The Columbia Jazz Band (jazz style)

Preparing for a Performance

Preparing for a performance takes careful planning and practice. Once a performance date is established, planning for that performance should begin immediately (assuming enough time has been scheduled in advance). A regular rehearsal schedule should be established. That schedule should include not only the times and dates of all rehearsals, it should also include an outline of what will be rehearsed at each practice. Review the information in this book about the rehearsal schedule.

A special rehearsal or set of rehearsals should be established just before the performance date. These are called the dress rehearsals because performers often do these practice sessions in conditions that equal or nearly equal those of the actual performance including wearing the same clothes that will be used for the performance. If possible, the dress rehearsals should be done in the same space in which you or your group will perform. This is important because the acoustics and character of each performance space is unique and it is helpful to get used to the "hall" before actually performing in it.

For your performance, make sure you have properly and more than adequately prepared your music but also consider how you will appear to your audience. Dress appropriate to the style and tradition of your music. Work to make an emotional connection to your audience. You are performing for them and not just for yourself (otherwise you could have just stayed home and played). Consider how you will present yourself to your audience. Also, consider what might distract your audience from appreciating your music. Avoid talking excessively or pointing out mistakes and shortcomings. Avoid distracting movements and motions unless they add to the performance itself.

Ensemble Performance Techniques

Ensemble Performance Elements
Accuracy
Musicality
Passion
Balance
Blend
Range

Successful techniques in performance for a musical ensemble are similar to the techniques for a solo performer but there are some additional things to consider. The three levels of successful performance: accuracy, shaping, and passion are equally applicable to performing groups but have to be true for a collection of musicians rather than just one. This fact creates additional challenges for an ensemble performance.

Ensemble Levels of Performance

Accuracy

All the members of the ensemble must be accurate in performing the notes and rhythms of the music. This requires not only that the group practice together to determine how these pitches and rhythms should be performed, but requires that each individual performer practice his or her own part to make sure that the part is performed accurately with the group. All members of the group must also have their instruments in tune and the group needs to also agree on a tuning pitch together. Performers must be both in tune with their own instrument as well as with the entire ensemble.

Musicality

The same holds true for the shaping of the music. The director decides or a group decision needs to be made about how the music will be shaped through dynamics, articulations, tempos, and phrasing. If such directions are indicated in the music, the director or group may choose to use them or alter them depending on the interpretation. Once the shaping decisions have been made and told to the group, each member of the group must practice his or her part to make sure he or she is playing with those prescribed shapings. Then, the whole group must practice to perform the shaped music together.

Passion

Finally, the energy level of the performance must be directed or agreed upon so that the group can do it as one ensemble. Just as in a solo performance the music must be analyzed for climactic points, intensity movements, and resolutions.

Additional Elements of Group Performance

Group Performance Elements
Balance
Blend
Range

Besides accuracy, shaping, and energy, there are some additional considerations that should go into a successful group performance. These factors are: balance, blend, and range.

Balance

Balance is achieved when the director or group determines which parts need to be heard over the others. It also involves making sure that all background parts are heard in a supportive role without being blocked out by the lead parts or other supportive parts. It helps to imagine a stage with performers on it in order to understand the concept of balance. Normally, instruments are put on a stage in such a way that the placement maximizes the balance of the group to the audience. Instruments put up front are meant to be heard the most. This is where the soloist or lead instruments are often placed while parts that are meant to support the lead are placed in the back. This is where we get the term "back-up instruments." The instruments in the back are often spread out evenly so that each part balances evenly with the other supporting parts.

Stage

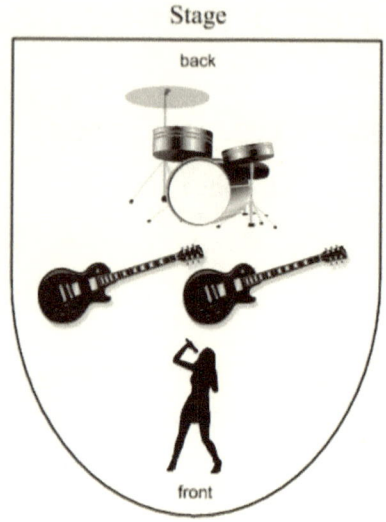

In the above example, the drums are placed in the rear of the stage because they are naturally very loud and could easily overpower the guitars and the vocalist. The two guitars are placed in the middle to balance with the drums but are behind the singer so as not to overpower him or her. The singer is placed up front with a microphone so that he or she can be easily heard over the drums and guitars. In considering the balance of all the instruments, volumes should be set to recreate a visual placement of instruments from front to back.

Blend

Blend is the ability to balance a musical ensemble in terms of dark versus bright tones. Each pitch made by any instrument can be played with a variety of tone qualities. Bright sounds contain a lot of harmonics. Bells and whistles are examples of typically bright sounds. Tones that are too "bright" can sound too "tinny" or "whistle-like." Dark sounds contain less harmonics. Low instruments and covered or muted instruments can sound dark. Tones that are overly dark can be called "muted" or "muddled." One of the jobs of a conductor or director is to try and get even and matched sounds from the performers. There may be times, depending on interpretation, when a bright or dark sound is needed but, for the most part, a balanced tone is often sought.

Range

Range is the distance from the highest sounding notes to the lowest sounding notes. In general, most good music performances will include both quite high sounds and quite low sounds. A director or group leader needs to make sure that all the sounds from the highest to the lowest and all the ranges in between can be heard fairly evenly. This is what you see when you watch an equalizer or audio bar on a control panel in a recording studio. Each vertical bar is a range of notes from low to high. Although each audio band may rise and fall, rarely does any one band stay far above or below for a long period of time.

Solo and Ensemble Evaluation Techniques

Evaluating Solo Performances

Solo Evaluation Elements
Accuracy
Shaping
Energy
Presentation
Overall

To evaluate the performance of individuals, consider how well a person has reached each of the three levels of performance.

In considering accuracy, the reviewer should determine whether or not the correct notes and rhythms were performed in accordance with the style of the music performed. For example, classical music requires an exact reproduction of the notes provided by the score. Contemporary and jazz music use fairly strict melodic formulas while allowing improvisation in the accompanying lines and certain sections of the form. Reviewers should also consider whether or not the performer's instrument was in tune and if the notes performed were in tune overall.

In considering musicality, the reviewer should determine what part the articulations, dynamics, tempos, and phrasing played in the overall effectiveness of the performance. The performer should have used all these things in the performance in an appropriate and effective way.

In evaluating passion, the reviewer should determine whether or not the performance had movement to it. There should have been at least one climactic point and that point should have been prepared and resolved through the performance. The reviewer should consider whether or not the performer attempted to reach out to the audience and make an emotional connection.

The reviewer should also consider the presentation made by the performer. He or she should be dressed in a manner that is appropriate to the style of the music and in a way that would enhance and not detract from the performance. Added sounds such as a loud tapping of the foot or the hands or other added motions may detract from the music itself. The performer might also talk excessively or say things that would affect the hearing of the music. The reviewer must take any extraneous noise or action into consideration when reviewing and decide if those things added to or took away from the performance.

In a final overview assessment, the reviewer should consider what worked well in the performance and what was not effective. The outline below will help with the performance review process.

Solo Performance Evaluation Checklist

- Accuracy
    - Were the notes played well?

- Were the rhythms played well?
- Were the notes and instrument in tune?
- Shaping
  - Were the articulations played well?
  - Were the dynamics played well?
  - Were the tempos and changes effective?
  - Was the phrasing effective?
- Energy
  - Was there musical movement in the performance?
    - expansions
    - climaxes
    - resolutions
  - Was there energy in the performance?
  - Did you experience an emotional expression?
- Presentation
  - Was the appearance appropriate?
  - Did the performer connect with the audience?
  - Did the performer do anything that distracted from the performance?
- Overall
  - What worked?

- What didn't work?

Evaluating Ensemble Performances

Ensemble Evaluation Elements
Accuracy
Shaping
Energy
Balance
Blend
Direction
Overall

Evaluating ensembles involves listening for many of the same things as solo performances but with some additional considerations.

Under accuracy, the reviewer needs to listen to whether or not all members of the ensemble played the correct notes and rhythms according to the style. All instruments need to be in tune with themselves but also with the ensemble as a whole. In shaping and energy as well, the reviewer needs to consider how well each individual performer contributed to the group and whether or not the net result was successful to the performance.

There are additional considerations already discussed relating to the evaluation of an ensemble and these are how well the ensemble was able to balance and blend with each other and how well they were led by a director. A complete checklist of these factors is provided below.

<u>Ensemble Performance Evaluation Checklist</u>

- Accuracy
    - Were the notes played well collectively?
    - Were the rhythms played well collectively?
    - Were the notes and instrument in tune with each other?
- Shaping
    - Were the articulations played well collectively?
    - Were the dynamics played well collectively?
    - Were the tempos and changes effective collectively?
    - Were the phrase effective collectively?
- Energy
    - Was there musical movement in the performance?
        - expansions
        - climaxes
        - resolutions
    - Was there collective energy in the performance?
    - Did you experience an emotional expression?
- Balance

- Were the volumes of the performers even and appropriate?

- Were the appropriate parts brought out?

- Was there a sense of acoustical spacing?

    - left to right

    - front to back

- Blend

    - Did the instruments evenly cover the sonic spectrum?

    - Did the performers match each others interpretations?

    - Did the tonal qualities work well together?

- Direction and Interaction

    - Did the ensemble have a focus and direction?

    - Did that direction lead to a good experience?

    - Did each member of the ensemble contribute equally to the performance?

    - Did they seem to get along well?

    - Did they seem to be enjoying themselves?

    - Did they connect with the audience?

- Overall

    - What worked?

- What didn't work?

Appendices

Performance Anxiety

One of the greatest obstacles to a successful performance–especially for young musicians–is performance anxiety. This is the frightful nervous feeling you get when you perform in front of a live audience. It is a perfectly natural fear to have, but it can be detrimental to performing with energy and connection. First, know that the fear of standing in front of a large group of people who are about to pass judgment on you is a very common one and almost all professional performers have had to come to grips with it in their careers. In fact, many never completely get over it. The feeling is basic and primal because it is based on the fear that you are vulnerable in a crowd of unfamiliar beings who may attack you at any moment. It helps to understand what your body is going through to learn how to deal with it.

Basically, your body is going into a fight-or-flight mode. Your adrenaline levels are increased so that you are ready to run away or defend yourself. Rising levels of this and other hormones throughout your body is why you get a dry mouth and the shakes among other physical responses. Other reactions include rapid heart rate, sweating, and shortness of breath. None of these reactions to stress is a problem in and of itself.

BEING NERVOUS IS NOT THE PROBLEM.

TRYING NOT TO BE NERVOUS IS THE PROBLEM.

In other words, stop worrying about being nervous. Your body is trying to help you by boosting your energy levels. Use that power reserve–channel it back into the music. When you try to stop being nervous, you expend even more energy trying to put down the rising energy levels already in your body. You will wear yourself out before you even start performing.

Trying not to be nervous is also a mental issue. For some reason, many believe that only amateurs get nervous while season-worn professionals are always calm and collected. This is simply not true. I have seen long-time professionals perform with their hands shaking. It is just that professionals know how to handle and use the pressure of performing to their advantage and they know how to hide the truth from their audiences. If you believe otherwise then you might be constantly and unnecessarily berating yourself every time you get stage fright.

There are many ways to deal with performance anxiety. One way is to take a type of drug called a beta-blocker. This type of medication blocks signals to beta receptors which, when stimulated, cause stress responses. These are powerful drugs and, like any medications, can come with side effects and complications. They should not be the first choice for performance anxiety relief; they should be the last. It is far better to try and deal with the anxiety through other methods such as through behavioral and cognitive techniques.

Another way to deal with performance anxiety is to learn techniques for relaxing your body as you accept and work with your own nervousness. An important part of being able to relax is in controlling the breath. Whenever we become frightened or anxious our breathing becomes short and shallow. Focusing on the breath while taking slow and full inhalations and exhalations can help control the body. Next time you feel nervous try this: take in a slow and full breath and then breathe out with rounded lips to slow the exhalation down. Do this until you feel more relaxed but stop if you start to feel light-headed. For more exercises, see the section below on Breathing Techniques.

One of the best and most musical ways to deal with performance anxiety is to learn to pull away from your own fears and focus solely on making music. Being a musical performer is like being an actor in that you have to get into the character and mood of the situation. When you perform music you should know it so well that it becomes a part of you. You should be very familiar with it to the point that you can understand its meaning and its message. Become the message and the emotion behind the work itself and lose yourself in that feeling. Athletes and others have experienced this in their practice until they no longer feel separate from what they are doing. Psychologists call this a "peak experience" or "being in a state of flow." Learn to lose yourself in your rehearsals and your performance and both you and your audience will have a greater overall experience.

Positive self-talk can be a powerful way to deal with performance anxiety. Many times performers are subject to criticism from peers, teachers, and themselves. Even if that criticism is meant to help the student, it can still lead to a self image that is less than positive. Sometimes it necessary to ignore all that and tell yourself things that are helpful. You have to believe in yourself or nobody else will. You do not have to be the best performer or the most perfect person in order to believe in yourself, either. Regardless of your level of ability you can believe in your dedicated effort to do better. You can believe in your goals and the reasons you have developed them. Find reasons to be positive about yourself and your goals. Tell yourself you CAN do it but also be patient with yourself to get it done. Before performing, tell yourself to do your best and be proud of your effort.

The main reason most performers lose confidence in their rehearsing and performing is because of negative self-talk. We are all our own worst critics and, depending on your experiences as a child, can be very hard on ourselves. There are four general destructive thinking patterns that affect most musicians: the All Or Nothing, Generalization, Filtering, and Should-ing.

In the All Or Nothing pattern, you think to yourself that everything must be perfect or you are a failure. It must be all good all the time or everything is all bad. It's an extreme way of thinking because there is no room for compassion or forgiveness. It ignores the reality that every person and every performance is imperfect. If everything was always perfect, it would be stale and sterile. Imperfection is not a bad thing.

With Generalization, one problem or mistake is overblown and then related to everything else. Words like always and never often reveal the presence of a generalization as do the words everyone or no one. You can hear these words in sentences like 'I never do that passage right' or 'I always miss that note' or 'everyone thinks I'm a failure.' A single instance–even if repeated–cannot define everything else. The future is not carved in stone. It is full of possibilities–including the possibility that you may do things better. If you tell yourself you will never be successful, you will close off your own range of possibilities and you will prove yourself to be correct. This will create a loop of negative thoughts and confirmations.

Filtering is the opposite of Generalization. With filtering, you focus on one negative thing and ignore all other information. Someone might say to you 'I thought you did a nice job on your solo' but you say 'It was terrible. I missed a note in the bridge.' You are so focused on the one note you miss that you ignore anything else you may have done well. You judge yourself by one mistake rather than the overall effectiveness of your performance.

Should-ing is when you tell yourself you should or shouldn't do something. Thoughts like: 'I should be able to do this' or 'I shouldn't make any mistakes' sets you to some kind of standard that may not be realistic. Of course you should have some standards and aspirations but those need to be tailored to the reality of your situation. You cannot expect to play like a professional after just one year of study. This is where setting reasonable long and short goals is important.

The way to defeat negative self-talk is to first recognize what you are telling yourself and when you do it. Then, challenge those thoughts. Does your performance really have to be perfect? Does this one problem really affect your entire performance, your future, your image of yourself? What things have you done well but chosen to ignore? Remind yourself of the following: It takes a lot of time, dedication, and hard work to develop as a musician. Even the best performers make mistakes and will always make mistakes, they just know how to work with or around them. You might never be the best performer but you are not the worst either. Mistakes are not bad things that determine your worth, they are the things that help you learn to do better.

Mental rehearsing is another method that can be used to think more positively about your performance. Find a way to be alone and relaxed for some time. In your mind, see yourself getting up to perform and then performing your pieces just as you would like them to be played. Go over the performance in your mind until it goes exactly as you would like.

Breathing Techniques

Many performance problems and playing issues stem from an inability to properly support breathing. This is especially true for instruments where the breath is a part of the tone like singing or playing wind instruments, but breathing is important for all musicians. Breathing properly can have three positive effects: calming the mind, calming the body, and making it possible to support a good musical tone.

To understand how to breath, you must understand how the respiratory system works. Your diaphragm muscle surround your lungs. To breathe in, the diaphragm lowers and expands into the regions of your stomach and intestines. The natural state of the lungs is to be mostly deflated. It takes more energy to inhale then exhale. When you exhale, the job of the diaphragm is to resist completely deflating the lungs all at once. In music, this action must be managed so that a steady flow of air can be put through the instrument. The inhalation needs to be as full as possible and the exhalation needs to be slow and controlled. To accomplish this you need good posture (sitting or standing) and control over the breathing process.

The lungs and the diaphragm

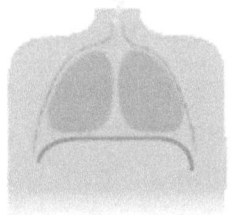

To learn to breath with an expanded and controlled breath, divide the breathing process into three parts: upper chest, middle chest (abdomen), and lower chest (waist). Each of these areas can be separately controlled. To identify these areas, lie down and put your hand on your chest. Place your thumb at your sternum (the place in the middle of your chest just below where the rib cage ends) and point the tip of your little finger toward your belly button. Your hand is now covering your middle chest area or the place where your abdominal muscles are located. See if you can breathe in by expanding only the upper chest area above your thumb. Next, practice expanding only the middle chest area. Finally, practice expanding only the lower chest area. The lower abdominal muscles in this area are the strongest and exert the most control over your breathing. Make sure you can feel and manipulate these muscles.

When you have mastered controlling each of these three separate areas, practice expanding each area in tandem. Start by expanding only the lower chest. Hold the lower chest in place as you expand the middle chest. Then hold the middle chest in place as you expand the upper chest. Exhale in the opposite manner, being careful to not release air in one area until released in the previous area. When this can be done easily, practice taking in a full breath that expands each of the three regions fully and evenly.

Increase the speed of this practice until you can take in a completely full breath in a short period of time.

The next step is to add this breathing technique to the performance of your instrument. Practice the quick breath but add a slow and controlled release of air after it. Use the muscles of the abdomen and ribs to keep the air from going out all at once. When you can do this play your instrument or sing single notes. Take in a full and complete breath then play or sing a sustained note for as long as you can. Learn to begin all your playing sessions by taking in a quick but full breath and then maintaining control over that air flow as your perform.

About the Author

Dr. Kenneth Langer is a published writer, composer, and poet. He has commercially published over 30 works of music, several poems, and two books on spirituality. He lives in the Boston area.

You can learn more about him and his books by looking through the following sites:

Personal Site:

http://kennethplanger.com

Book Site:

http://brassbellbooks.com

Email:

ken.langer@me.com

If you enjoyed reading this book please consider writing a positive review on Amazon or other online book sites.

Other Books by Kenneth P. Langer

Non-Fiction

- Spirituality
  - A Different Calling
    - A Manual for Lay Ministers and Other Non-Professional Facilitators of Any Spiritual Tradition
  - Many Leaves, One Tree
    - A Collection of Aphorisms Inspired by the Tao Te Ching
  - The Purpose Derived Life: What In The Universe Am I Here For?
  - Three Guidelines for Ethical Living: What My Daughter Taught Me
  - Prayers for a Postmodern World
  - Playing Cards and the Game of Living Well
- Games
  - 52 New Card Games (For Those Old Cards)
  - 36 New Dice Games
- Music
  - A Guide to the Art of Musical Performance

- A Theory for All Music
  - Book 1: Fundamentals
  - Book 2: Chords and Part-Writing
  - Book 3: The Tools of Analysis
  - Book 4: Parametric Analysis

Fiction

- Science Fiction
  - The Milleran Cluster Series
    - Of Eternal Light
    - The Forever Horizon
    - The Suicide Fire
    - The Song of the Mother
    - The Journey of Awri
- Theater
  - Four Comedies
  - 10 x 10: Ten Ten-Minute Plays - Book One
  - 10 x 10: Ten Ten-Minute Plays - Book Two
- Poetry
  - Looking At The World: A Collection of Poetry

About the Author

www.ingramcontent.com/pod-product-compliance
Lightning Source LLC
Chambersburg PA
CBHW021907170526
45157CB00005B/2010